BOOK 1

CHRISTIAN HITS for TEENS

W9-AIO-433

8 GRADED SELECTIONS
FOR EARLY INTERMEDIATE TO INTERMEDIATE PIANISTS
ARRANGED BY MELODY BOBER

Each generation has its unique style of musical worship to immerse individuals in praise and thanksgiving. Such music helps increase faith and leads toward a closer walk with God. Soulful melodies can extol God's love, provision, and comfort, and lyrics can touch hearts.

Christian Hits for Teens contains solo piano arrangements that students from this generation will recognize and enjoy learning. These familiar praise and worship songs, with their rhythmic vitality and rich harmonies, will especially appeal to teens. Students will enjoy performing these pieces at youth groups, camps, and in other church settings.

CONTENTS

ALFRED

Produced by
Alfred Music
P.O. Box 10003
Van Nuys, CA 91410-0003
alfred.com

Printed in USA.

ISBN-10: 1-4706-1119-8
ISBN-13: 978-1-4706-1119-4

ABOVE ALL

Words and Music by
Paul Baloche and Lenny LeBlanc
Arr. Melody Bober

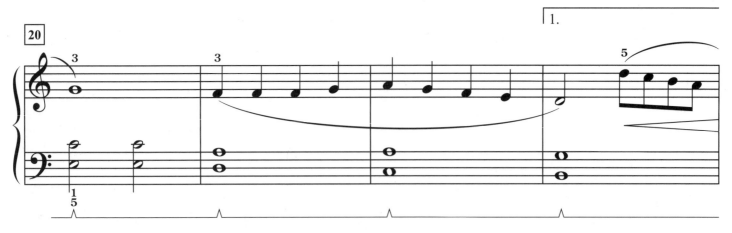

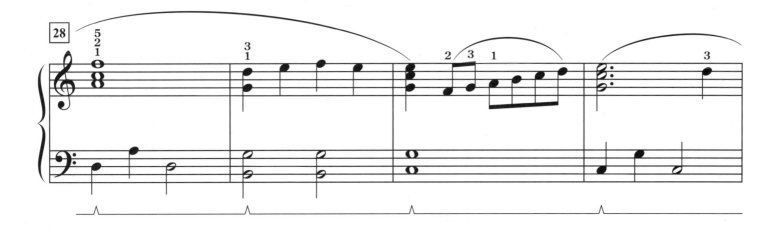

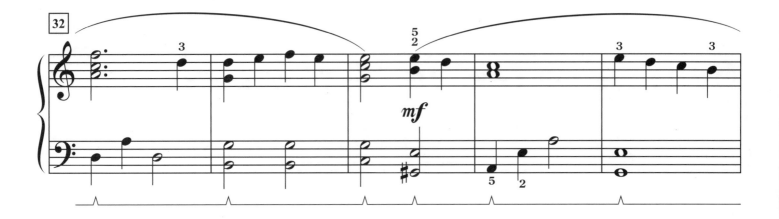

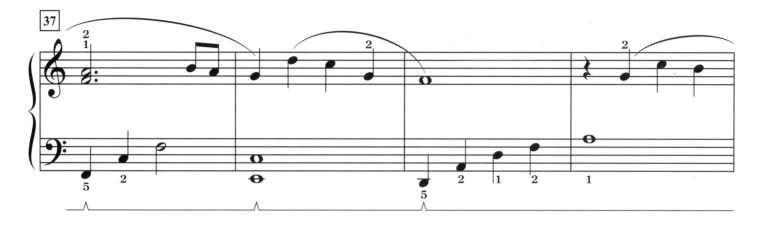

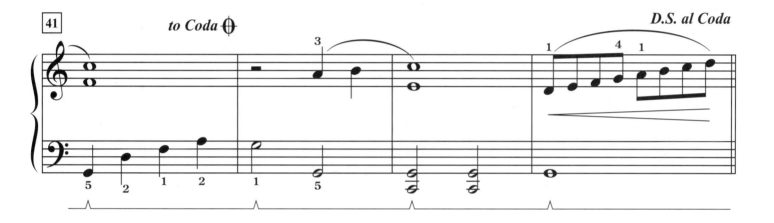

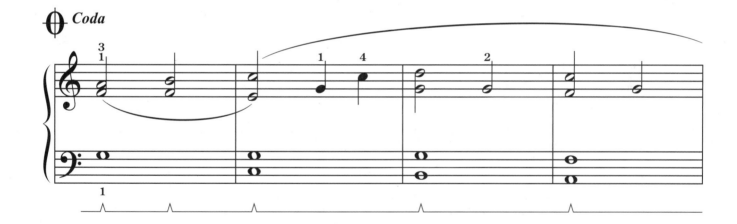

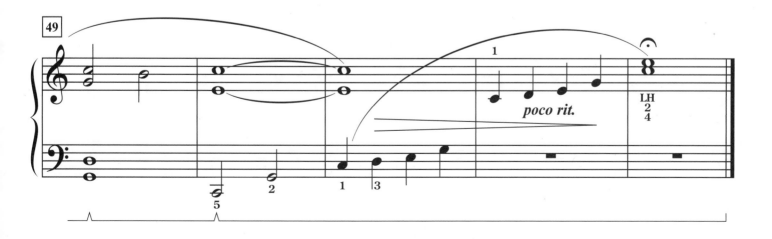

BLESSINGS

Words and Music by Laura Mixon Story
Arr. Melody Bober

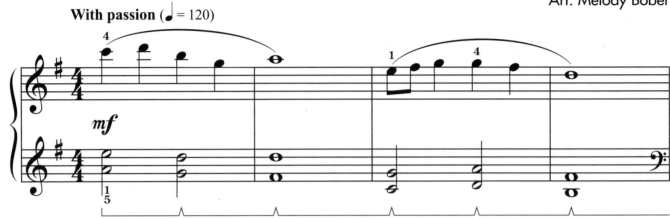

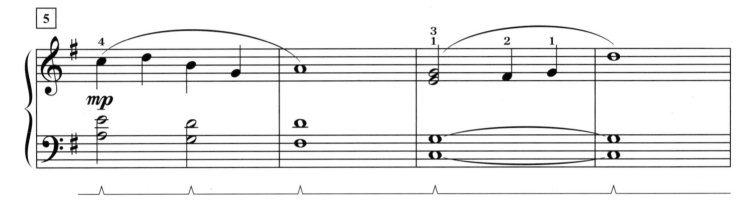

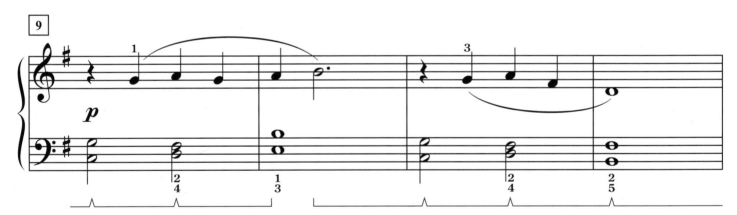

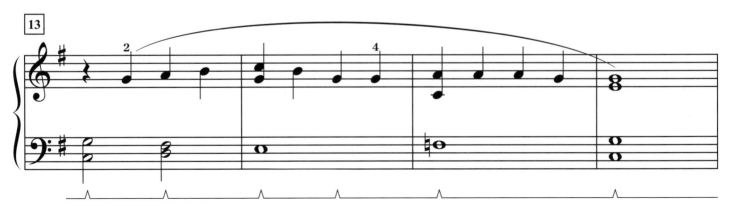

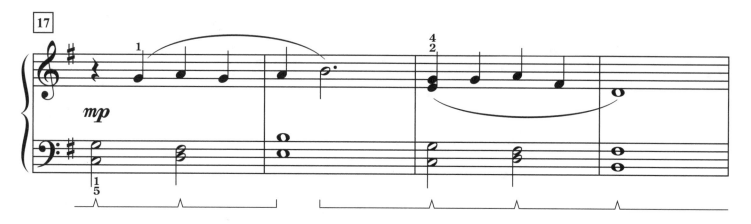

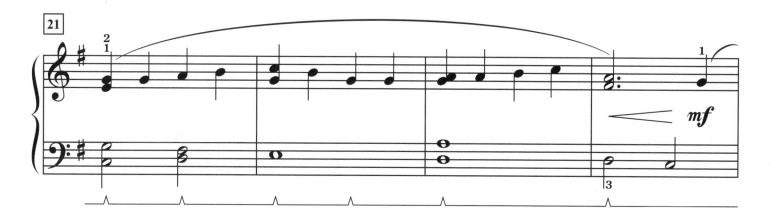

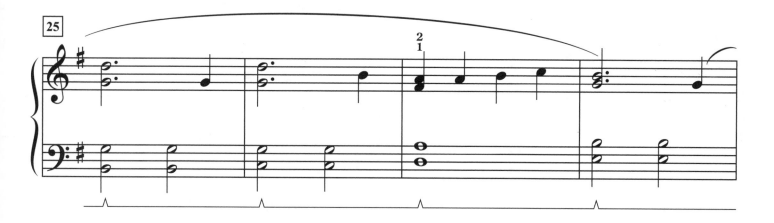

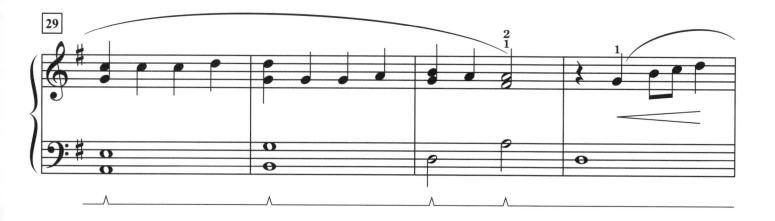

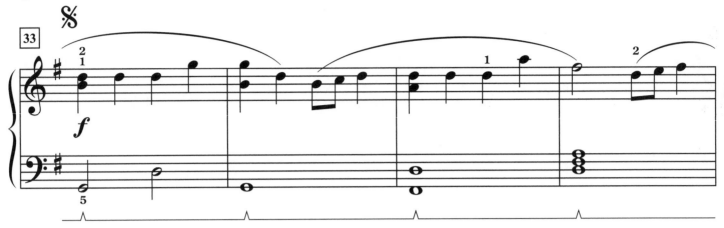

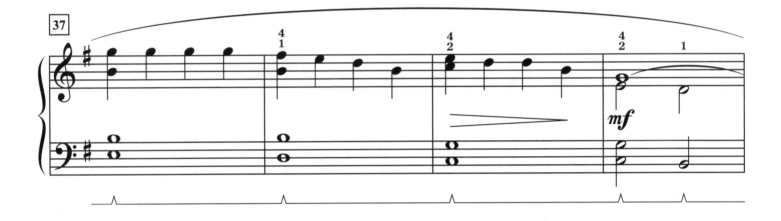

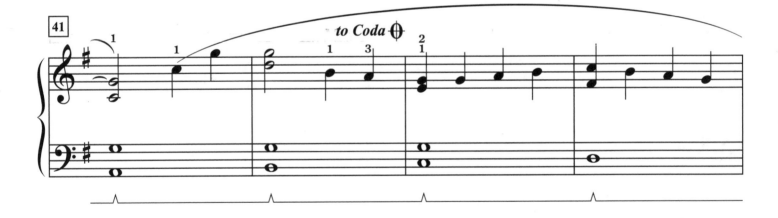

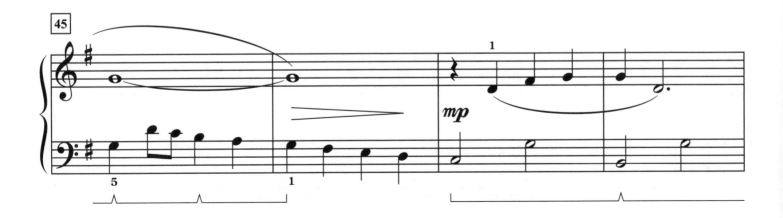

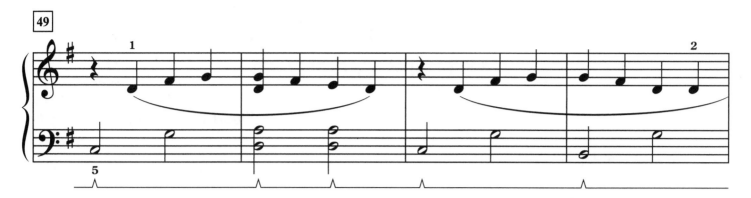

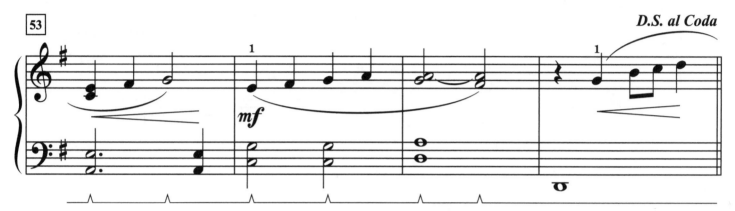

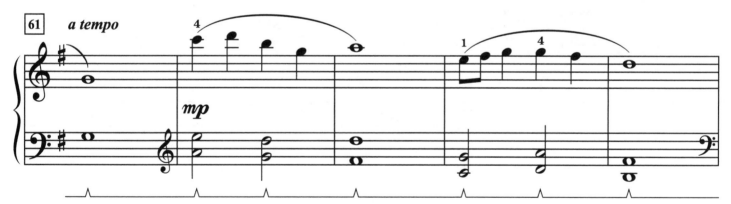

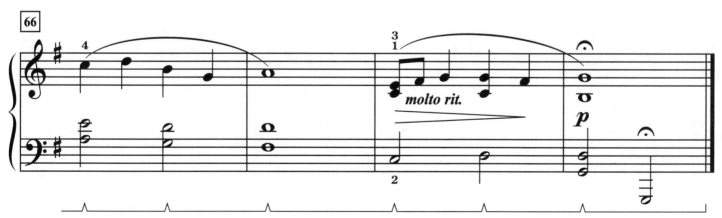

IN CHRIST ALONE
(MY HOPE IS FOUND)

Words and Music by
Stuart Townend and Keith Getty
Arr. Melody Bober

Praising Him (♩ = 76)

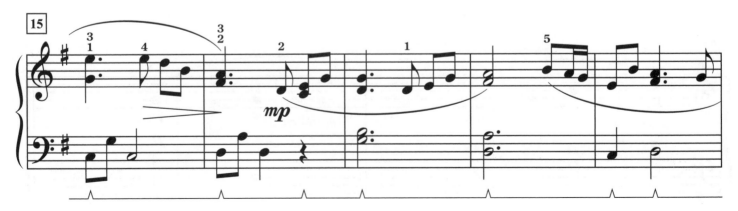

I NEED A MIRACLE

Words and Music by David Carr, Mac Powell,
Mark Lee and Tai Anderson
Arr. Melody Bober

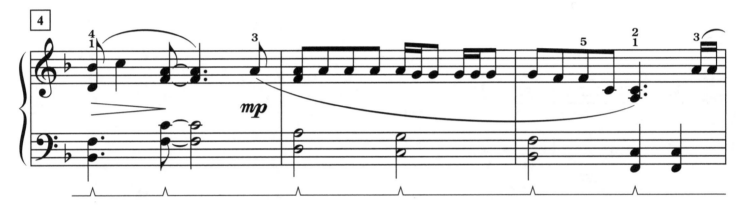

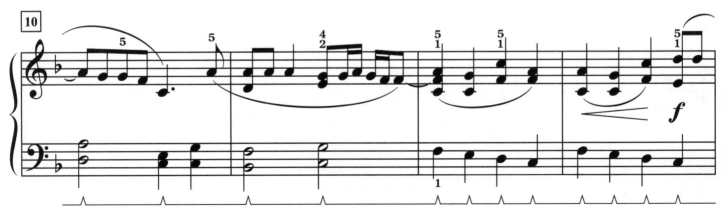

13

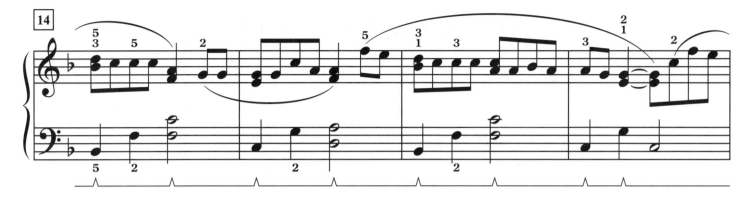

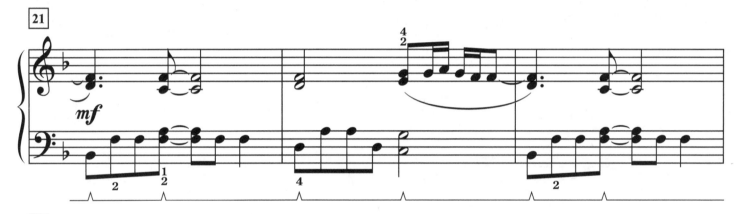

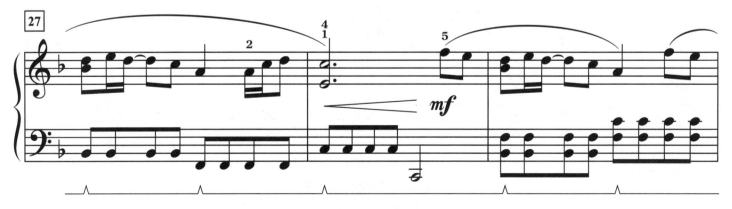

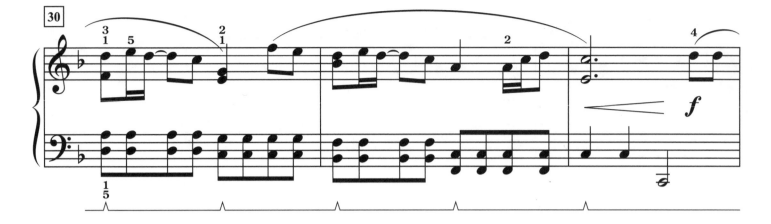

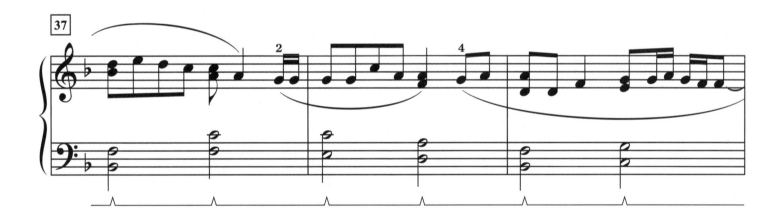

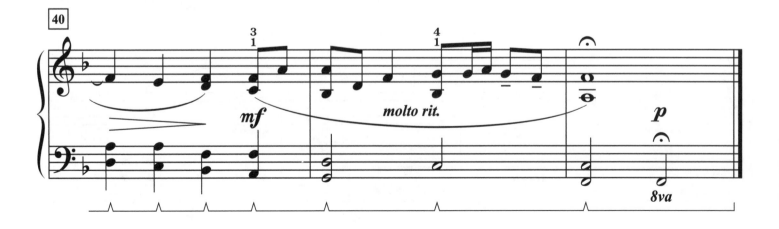

JESUS, FRIEND OF SINNERS

Words and Music by
Matthew West and Mark Hall
Arr. Melody Bober

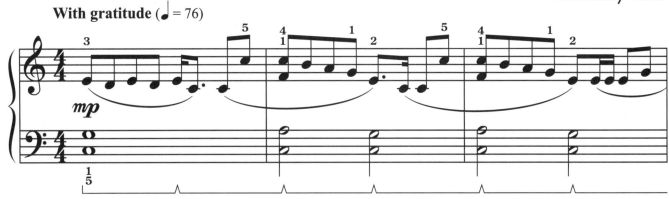

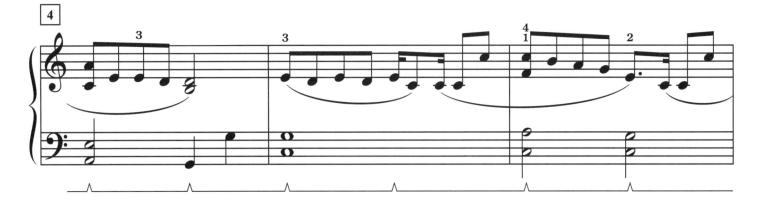

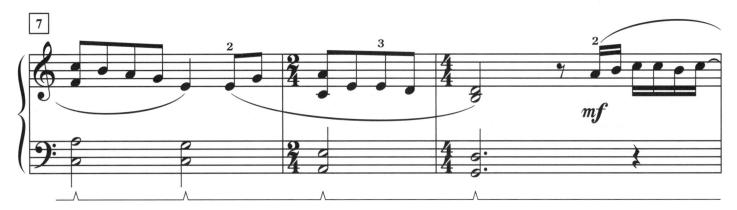

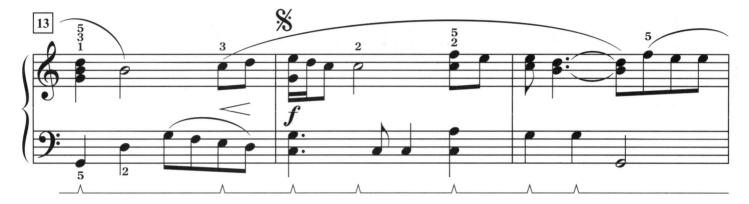

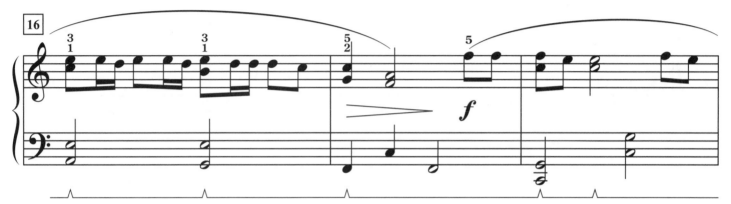

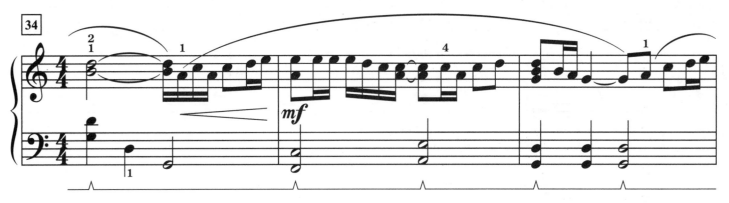

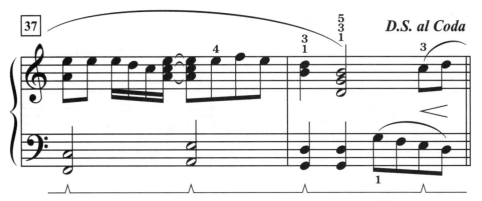

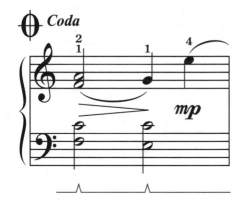

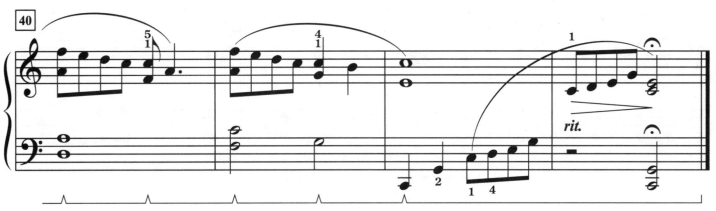

SHOUT TO THE LORD

Words and Music by Darlene Zschech
Arr. Melody Bober

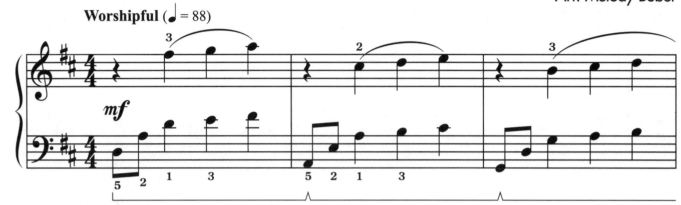

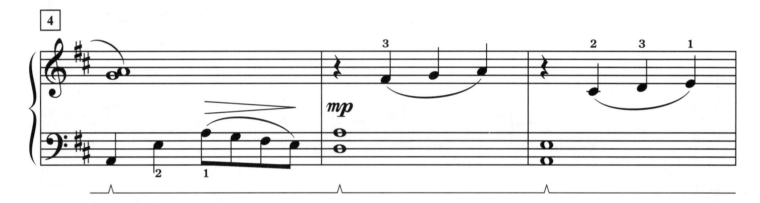

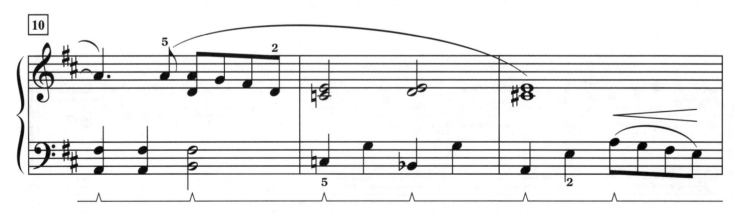

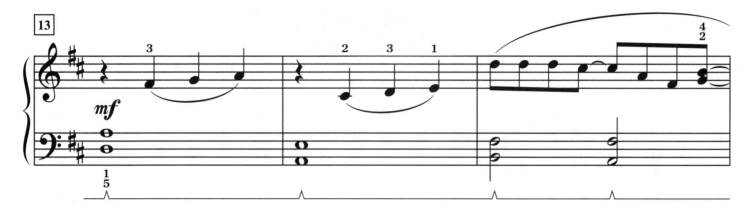

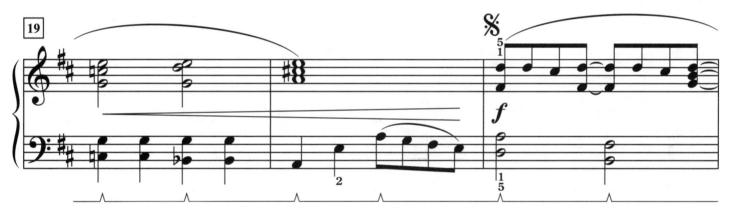

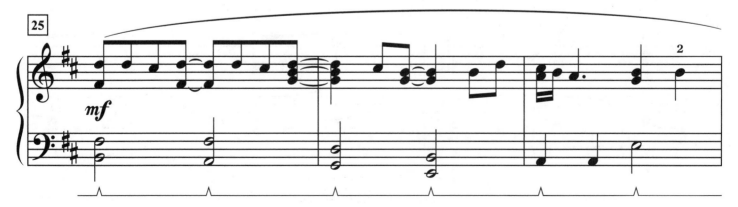

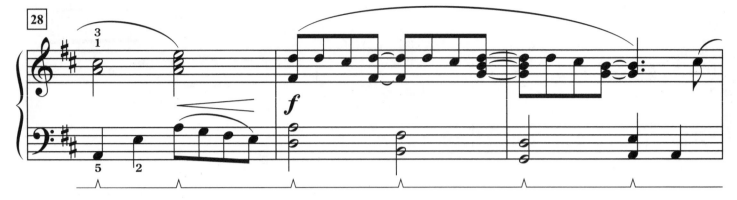

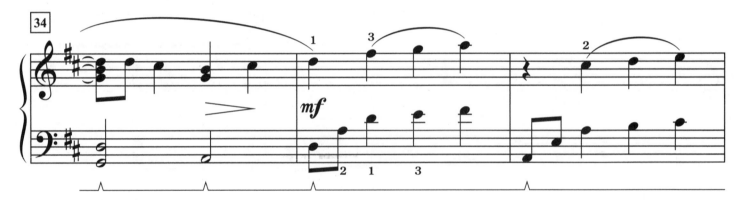

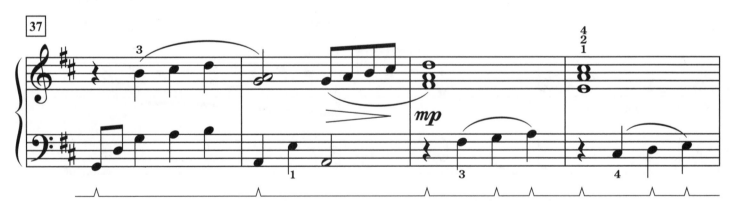

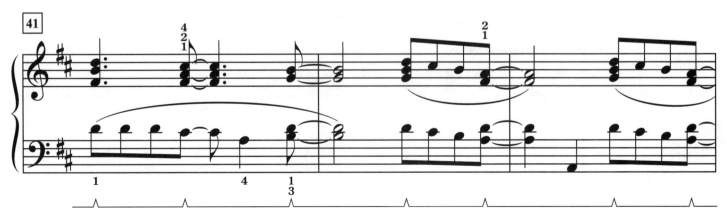

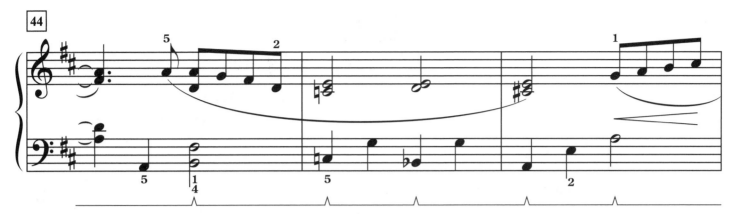

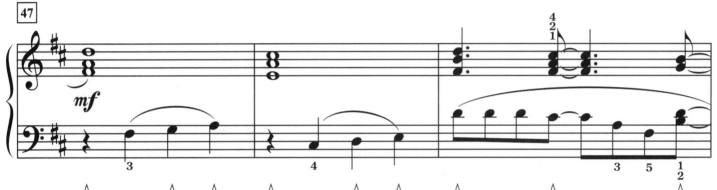

D.S. al Coda

Coda

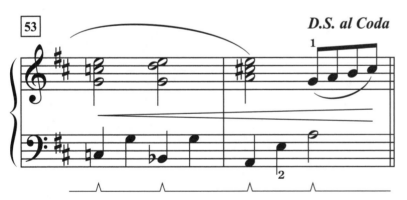

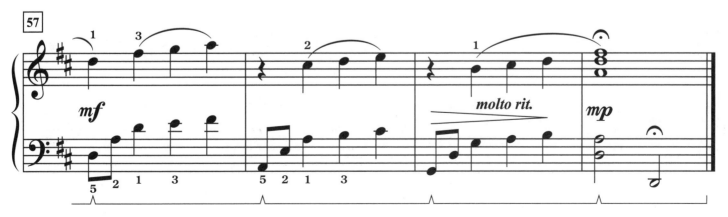

molto rit.

WE ARE

Words and Music by Ed Cash, Chuck Butler,
James Tealy and Hillary McBride
Arr. Melody Bober

With energy ($\quarternote$ = 120)

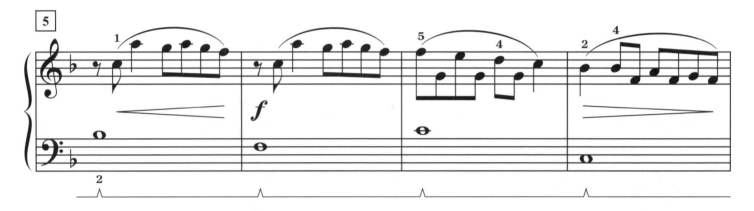

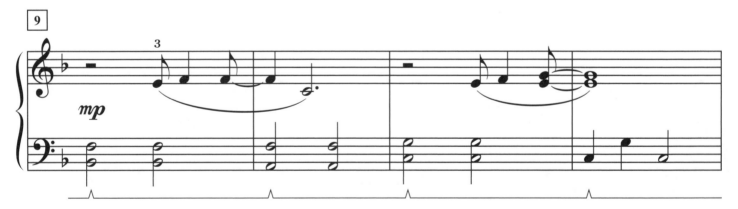

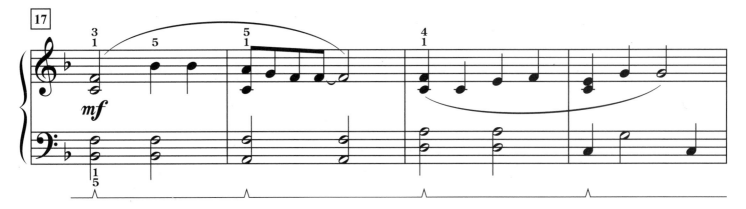

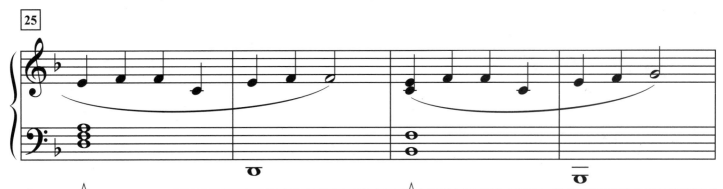

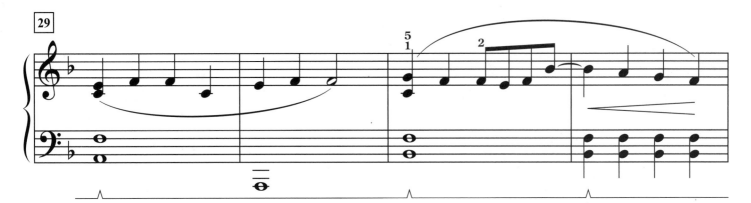

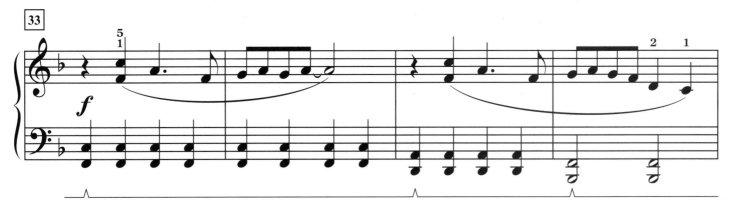

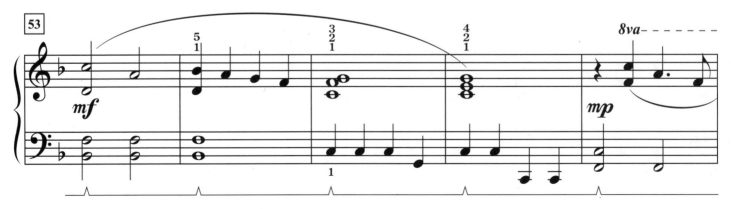

WHOM SHALL I FEAR
(GOD OF ANGEL ARMIES)

Words and Music by Chris Tomlin,
Ed Cash and Scott Cash
Arr. Melody Bober

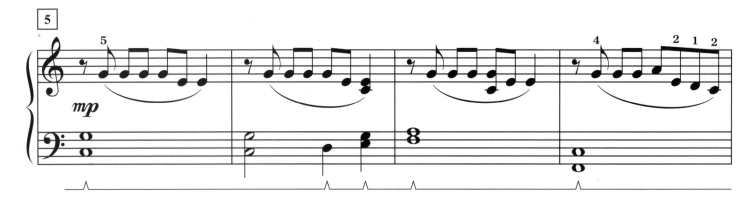

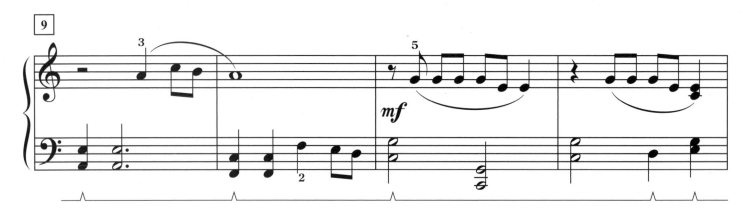

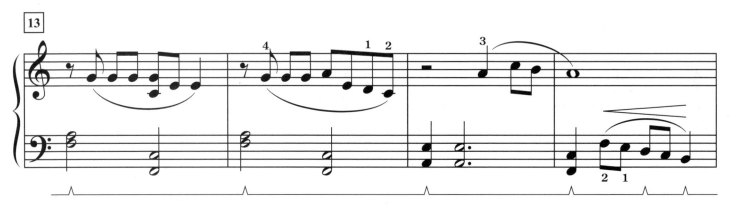

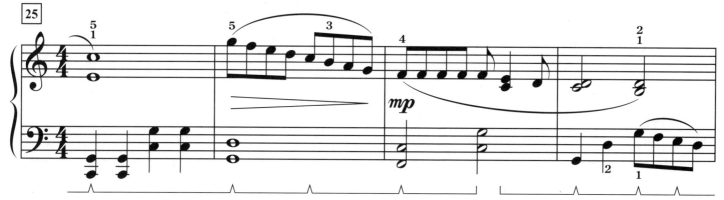

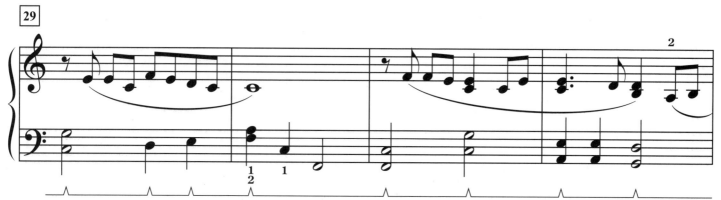

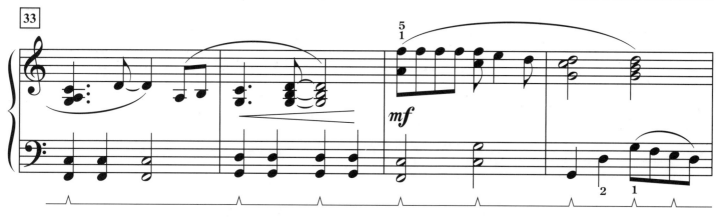

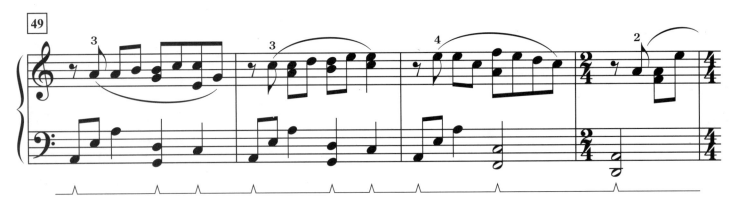

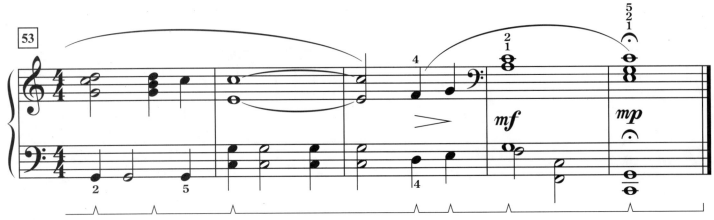